Printed in Great Britain
by Amazon

82982768R10066